Issues with Big Data Analytics – As It Is

(Search for NextGen Storage Material – DNA Data Warehouse)

ISBN 978-1-326-23637-3

Contents

Introduction

With growing dependency on IT, where IT is needed in every sphere of life these days, the elementary unit that gets processed with computing i.e. data is growing at exponential rate, which has given birth to term big data.

Data or the information is most basic or critical part on which any computing function relies, with advancements and researches there have been growth in new algorithms, functions and sophisticated systems but the data i.e. churned through these systems is cause of concern for future, the data is growing everyday with frequency more than millions of bytes every second, the storage retrieval and processing is becoming challenging.

Following are challenges related to big data at very fundamental level:-

1) Storage.

2) Retrieval.

3) Processing.

Big Data at high level may look like a problem only for research or data extensive computing such as aviation and space science but at minute level big data actually impacts each one of us.

The problem may not look as big as it is speculated currently but with every detail of whole population of earth being captured in form of data, the Big Data will be a big problem, there are many approaches that shows how can we effectively manage big data, though it is very important to understand difference between big data and regular data.

The data is basic building block of any information system and if the information system doesn't carry the capability to store, process and retrieve the amount of data we need, the system will be of no use.

Not adopting to systems that are able to process big data will no longer be a choice in near future, this can be seen from the fact that, how much information do we all process in one day, starting from the alarm tone from the latest mobile phone, every morning, to reading newspaper on the 3G capable mobile phone, logging on and checking social networking sites and work e-mails, on an average we can assume, a person working in non-IT job would be processing minimum of 1 GB of information

If someone doesn't uses mobile phones or latest gadgets, still if he is travelling through a public transport system or a car, or even if withdrawal or deposit is done in a bank or ATM, information is processed.

In short, we all are the part of problem, the solution to problem is definitely not simple, it does need lot of thought and research, every IT organization is coming up with a solution to process big data, the problem still lies beyond, i.e. the data can be stored, data can be processed and retrieved easily, the latest research and techniques prove to process very large volumes of data in just fraction of minutes but the larger part of problem is still unexplored i.e. where will the data be stored.

Chapter 1

Source of Big Problem

In introduction, very briefly, it has been explained from where did the problem of exponentially increasing data is emerging, let's explore further to understand this in more details.

Big data is collection of large and complex data sets. Average size of big data can be realized to 1000 terabyte.

With the growing information system where information of everything about us and around us is captured in electronic form and stored and needs to be ready for retrieval anytime we want.

The data is growing at exponential rate. This is leading to "Big Data".

Problem around information systems dealing with Big Data is not only limited to storage of information, it extends to retrieval, analysis, presentation and modification of the data.

Following are the few areas where Big Data processing can cause issue.

1) Medical.

2) Defence.

3) Metrology.

4) Space Research.

5) Business and Banking applications.

6) Government applications and census.

The list is not exhaustive but the big data storage and retrieval is cause of concern for future for any information system we can think of and there are any approaches that have been advised and are currently being followed to solve the data processing issues.

Following are few examples that explain the need of increasing storage space:

1) Genome Sequencing

Human genome takes around 3 Gb of storage space, for the researches in genetic science, it is very important to get sequence of full human genome.

Human genome information is used for development of vaccination, disease prediction in an individual and drug development.

Further, there can be a time where we need to sequence genome for every human or possibly every organism in such a case if we have 7 billion people on earth then we need 21 billion Gb of storage space.

2) Banking and Finance Applications

Any bank in this world on average has more than 1 million customers and if we average information of each customer to 100 Mb each then we are currently using 1 million Gb of storage space and the new systems that are getting evolved as per the market trends will be increasing this capacity to 100 times.

3) Social networking Websites

There are million users on social networking sites and if each user uploads 500 personal photos on the social networking website each year and if each photo is of size 2 Mb then we can say that social networking sites need to increase the storage space by 1Gb each user each year.

4) Government and Census applications

In the current trend of information where each country is trying to get all information from census, taxes and customs etc. in paper less form, we can realize that information of every individual will be around 500 Mb in data terms there is a direct proportion over here, which means if the population will increase, the data will also increase and hence the storage needs.

5) Space Research

Space research missions such as mission on planet Mars would require several million Gb of storage space and with increase in exploration of space, the needs of increasing storage space will always be increasing.

Solution to all problems is that there should be enough storage material in this world to save all the information processed by all information systems in the universe.

Chapter 2

Storage mediums and NeXT Generation Solution

Following are the commonly used storage mediums:

1) Semiconductor e.g. semiconductor devices such as transistors and capacitors.

2) Magnetic e.g. magnetic tapes and hard disk drives.

3) Optical e.g. CD, DVD etc.

The important thing to note here is that there is no upper limit for increasing storage space; the need to increase storage space will always be there.

After digging into problem and getting to know the serious problem of growing storage needs. It is very clear that we need a next generation material to cater for big data storage.

We need a material that is available in large quantities and will never be exhausted.

Availability is one of the most important factors while looking for the Next generation solution for storage material, other than availability. The material should have material properties similar to existing storage materials that are widely used such as silicon, i.e. it should have retention and material strength.

If we look around the available materials, we can get many materials which have properties similar to silicon and can be used for storage but will be in limited quantities, the best material that can be used for such a purpose could be DNA.

To meet with the demands of increasing storage, we definitely need to adopt new storage technology or storage material that should be available in large quantities and also must cost less.

The possible future technology is to use DNA as a storage medium.

Reiterating that the DNA is basic material for any life on earth, DNA stores genetic information which is passed from parents to offspring.

The DNA is information or data storage unit for life, the question now arise is that can we use DNA to store the data that we want, can we use DNA to store string of characters.

This sounds challenging, at first instance, however, if we give it thought then information is just the arrangement of bits.

If we drill down for structure of DNA, it can be seen that in DNA is built up from nucleotides, i.e. Adenine (A), Thymine (T), Cytosine(C) and Guanine (G).

The basis of this approach is that if by arrangement of bits i.e. 0's and 1's we can represent data or information, then we can do same with arrangement of A, T, G and C as well.

Chapter 3

Why Select DNA

Motive of selecting nucleotide of DNA to represent information is very clear.

If we look around ourselves, the thing that is most abundant around us is DNA. It's the storage material i.e. there in every living thing, whether its plants, humans, animal or reptile.

Further, the structure of DNA is quite stable and it can easily be engineered, i.e. it can be modified as per our needs.

Naturally DNA structure is varied due to mutation and in lab conditions.

We can modify the structure using site directed mutagenesis, which is a technology that helps us to modify the DNA as we want.

DNA is usually a double stranded DNA, where one strand is named as 3'→5' strand and other is named as 5'→3' strand. For our purpose, i.e. for data representation, we will be using 3'→5' strand only.

Deoxyribonucleic acid or more commonly known as DNA is a molecule that contains genetic instructions that is carried from one generation to another.

Since DNA is a building block of cell, it is available in all living objects and is available in large quantities.

Chapter 4

DNA Structure and DNA Processing

Since, we are more concerned for using DNA as a storage material rather than a code for building up the proteins. It is worthwhile to understand the structure of the DNA.

DNA is a double stranded helices structure, it is made of two chains of nucleotides, which in turn is made up of nucleobase, alternating sugar and the phosphate group, nucleobase are characterised as following:-

A – Adenanine

T – Thymine

G – Guanine

C – Cytosine

The two chains of nucleotide correspond to each other, i.e. they run anti-parallel.

The direction of the chain or also known as strand is marked by the prime, it is starting and ending with.

One strand runs from 3'(three prime) to 5' (five prime) and other strand runs from 5'(five prime) to 3'(three prime), as shown below:-

DNA is a long polymer, containing millions of nucleotides.

DNA usually does not exist as a single molecule but the multiple molecules that are held tightly together.

The repeating nucleotides are linked to a sugar and the phosphate base.

DNA double helix is a highly stable material, it is stabilized by following two molecular forces:-

1) Hydrogen bonds between nucleotides:-

Hydrogen bond is a pseudo bond, it is actually dipole attraction i.e. electromagnetic attractive attractions between polar molecules i.e. bond between, hydrogen (H) and nitrogen (N), oxygen (O) or fluorine (F).

The hydrogen bond can be intermolecular or intramolecular, the hydrogen bonds are weaker than the covalent bonds. Hydrogen bond has been found responsible for the following material characteristics:-

- High boiling point of water (H_2O).

- High melting point and viscosity.

- High solubility of some compounds in water.

- Density - ice is less dense than liquid water is due to a crystal structure stabilized by hydrogen bonds.

Most important material characteristic that is explained by the hydrogen bond is temperature stability; hydrogen bonding is stable only over the range of temperature known as "anomaly temperature".

This also explains how, the DNA, double helix structure is not stable at high temperature.

Hydrogen bonding happens when the hydrogen is attached directly to one of the most electronegative elements, causing the hydrogen to acquire a significant amount of positive charge.

Each of the elements (N, O, F) to which the hydrogen is attached is not only significantly negative, but also has at least one "active" lone pair.

Lone pairs at the 2-level have the electrons contained in a relatively small volume of space which therefore has a high density of negative charge.

Lone pairs at higher levels are more diffuse and not so attractive to positive things.

2) Molecular interactions among the nucleobase.

- The nucleobase, based on their structure can be classified into two types at high level:-

- Purines (A and G) – These are five and six member hetrocycle compounds.

- Pyrimidine (C, T and U)– These are six member rings.

- Uracil(U) exists only in RNA and doesn't exist in DNA.

Base Pairing

DNA double helix results from molecular interactions between, Purine (A and G) and Pyrimidine (T and C).

This is called complimentary base pairing, where purines form hydrogen bonds to pyrimidines, with adenanine(A) bonding to thymine(T) in two hydrogen bonds and cytosine(C) bonding only to guanine(G) in three hydrogen bonds.

Base pairing is due to hydrogen bonds between purines and pyrimidine, since hydrogen bonds are unstable at high temperature, the double helix structure or base pairing is also unstable at high temperature.

Physiologically base pairing is important as it actually replicates information on one strand onto the other strand.

Guanine(G) and Cytosine(C) bonding is stronger than Adenine(A) and Thymine(T) bond.

There are two hydrogen bonds between Adenine(A) and Thymine(T) and three hydrogen bonds between Guanine(G) and Cytosine(C).

So the material strength/stability of the DNA depends on GC-content i.e. % GC base pairs.

In the laboratory, the strength of this interaction can be measured by finding the temperature necessary to break the hydrogen bonds.

When all the base pairs in a DNA double helix melt, the strands separate and exist in solution as two entirely independent molecules.

In DNA a strand circles the axis of the double helix once every 10.4 base pairs.

For stability the DNA is tightly twisted to forma super coil structure.

If the DNA is twisted in the direction same as helix, this is termed as positive supercoiling, in such a case bases are held more tightly, if the DNA is twisted in opposite direction to helix, this is negative supercoiling and the bases come apart more easily.

With use of some enzymes, DNA can be made from positive supercoiling to negative supercoiling or vice-versa.

There are other forms of the DNA that are also known for e.g. multi branched DNA, Z-DNA etc. but for using as a storage material, we will be ignoring those DNA structures.

Chapter 5

DNA Extraction and Sequencing

In any living being, DNA exists inside chromosome, it is binded by structural proteins. A distinct group of DNA-binding proteins are the DNA-binding proteins that specifically bind single-stranded DNA.

DNA extraction is done through chemical and mechanical treatment. It involves, breaking the cell, i.e. cell disruption or cell lysis, removing the proteins, filtering DNA from the suspense.

Purification of DNA is done by using alcohol, as the DNA is insoluble in alcohols, it aggregates together upon centrifugation with alcohol.

Refinements of the technique include adding a chelating agent to sequester divalent cations such as Mg2+ and Ca2+, which prevents enzymes like DNase from degrading the DNA.

Cellular and histone proteins bound to the DNA can be removed either by adding a protease or by having precipitated the proteins with sodium or ammonium acetate, or extracted them with a phenol-chloroform mixture prior to the DNA-precipitation.

After isolation, the DNA is dissolved in slightly alkaline buffer, in the TE buffer, or in distilled water.

After extraction, it is essential to know the sequence of nucleotides inside the DNA, DNA sequencing is the process of determining the precise order of nucleotides within a DNA molecule.

It includes any method or technology that is used to determine the order of the four bases—adenine, guanine, cytosine, and thymine—in a strand of DNA.

The advent of rapid DNA sequencing methods has greatly accelerated biological and medical research and discovery.

Knowledge of DNA sequences has become indispensable for basic biological research, and in numerous applied fields such as diagnostic, biotechnology, forensic biology, and biological systematics.

The rapid speed of sequencing attained with modern DNA sequencing technology has been instrumental in the sequencing of complete DNA sequences, or genomes of numerous types and species of life, including the human genome and other complete DNA sequences of many animal, plant, and microbial species.

Chapter 6

Proposed Method

The 3'→5' strand of DNA will be engineered in different sections as per the need. The strands will be characterized, in four sections, database name, table name, attribute name and values.

DNA can be extracted from any living thing, for e.g. a leaf of a plant and small fragments of high molecular DNA can be achieved by chain termination method and by shotgun sequencing method.

Following table represents how the different sections of the strands will be represented.

	Starts With	Ends With
Data-Base Name	G	C
Table Name	C	G
Attribute Name	G	G
Value	C	C

Identification of strand 3'→5' will be done on basis it is starting with nucleotide 'G'.

However, the corresponding, 5'→3' strand will be starting with nucleotide 'C'.

Once, we have enough storing material i.e. DNA in place, we can achieve the DNA strand that we require, using the technique site directed mutagenesis, i.e. we can make a DNA strand which starts with G and after that with combinations of

'A' and 'T' we can represent a database, entity and attribute name.

- Sample DNA representations

Let us take an example, where following are the names of database, entity, attribute and values.

<u>Data-Base Name</u>: EmpDb

<u>Table Name</u>: Employee

Name	Age
Abc	25
Xyz	36

Following DNA strand of 344 nucleotide sequence represents the table above:-

3'GATAAATATATTATTATATTTAAAAATAAATAAAT
TAAATACCATAAATATATTATTATATTTAAAAATTAT
TAAATTATTTTATTTTAATATTAATATATTAATATGG
ATAATTTAATTAAAATATTATTATATTAATATGCATT
AAAATATTAAATAATTAAATTCCATTTTAAAATTTTA
ATATTTTATACGATAAAAATATTAATTTATTAATATG
CAATTAATAAATTATATCCAATTAATTAATTATTACC
ATTAAAATATTAAATAATTAAATTCCATTTTAAAATT
TTAATATTTTATACCAATTAATAAATTATATCCAATT
AATTAATTATTAC'5

The addition and modification of entity/attributes/values can be done, in the naming convention above. The DNA strand can be as long or as short, depending upon the requirements.

For the purpose of stability, we need the DNA strand to be double stranded, i.e. we require corresponding 5'→3' strand as well.

The 5'→3' strand will be represented as following:-

5'CTATTTATATAATAATATAAATTTTTATTTATTTAA
TTTATGGTATTTATATAATAATATAAATTTTTAATAA
TTTAATAAAATAAAATTATAATTATATAATTATACCT
ATTAAATTAATTTTATAATAATATAATTATACGTAAT
TTTATAATTTATTAATTTAAGGTAAAATTTTAAAATT
ATAAAATATGCTATTTTTATAATTAAATAATTATACG
TTAATTATTTAATATAGGTTAATTAATTAATAATGGT
AATTTTATAATTTATTAATTTAAGGTAAAATTTTAAA
ATTATAAAATATGGTTAATTATTTAATATAGGTTAAT
TAATTAATAATG**'3**

While we are inserting data to table, we need to append 3'→5' and 5'→3' both.

- **Lab Procedures**

The lab procedure includes basically three steps:-

1) Extraction of DNA.

2) Sequencing of DNA.

3) Site Directed changes/mutagenesis.
The process flow is shown below:-

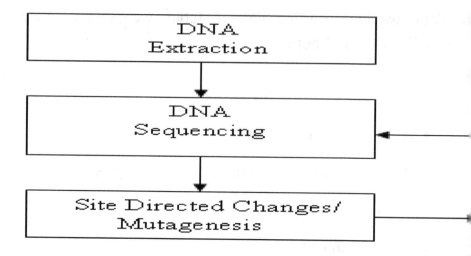

Step 2 and Step3 needs to be run till the final strand of 3'→5' and 5'→3' DNA is not achieved.

Manually performing this activity can take lot of time but however, in the world where we have robotic arms and other programmable devices, this process may not take longer.

- **Script for DNA analysis**

#Database Name

oriString = 'EmpDb'

fString = bin(reduce(lambda x, y: 256*x+y, (ord(c) for c in oriString), 0))

fString = fString.replace('1','T')

fString = fString.replace('0','A')

fString = 'G' + fString + 'C'

#Table Name

OriString = 'Employee'

fString = fString + bin(reduce(lambda x, y: 256*x+y, (ord(c) for c in oriString), 0))

fString = fString.replace('1','T')

```python
fString = fString.replace('0','A')

fString = 'C' + fString + 'G'


#Attribute Name


OriString = 'Name'

fString = fString + bin(reduce(lambda x, y: 256*x+y, (ord(c)
for c in oriString), 0))

fString = fString.replace('1','T')

fString = fString.replace('0','A')

fString = 'G' + fString + 'G'


#Value

OriString = 'abc'

fString = fString + bin(reduce(lambda x, y: 256*x+y, (ord(c)
for c in oriString), 0))
```

```python
fString = fString.replace('1','T')

fString = fString.replace('0','A')

fString = 'C' + fString + 'C'


#Value

OriString = 'xyz'

fString = fString + bin(reduce(lambda x, y: 256*x+y, (ord(c)
for c in oriString), 0)))

fString = fString.replace('1','T')

fString = fString.replace('0','A')

fString = 'C' + fString + 'C'



#Attribute Name

OriString = 'Age'
```

```python
fString = fString + bin(reduce(lambda x, y: 256*x+y, (ord(c) for c in oriString), 0))

fString = fString.replace('1','T')

fString = fString.replace('0','A')

fString = 'G' + fString + 'G'


#Value

OriString = '25'

fString = fString + bin(reduce(lambda x, y: 256*x+y, (ord(c) for c in oriString), 0))

fString = fString.replace('1','T')

fString = fString.replace('0','A')

fString = 'C' + fString + 'C'
```

```
#Value

OriString = '36'

fString = fString + bin(reduce(lambda x, y: 256*x+y, (ord(c)
for c in oriString), 0))

fString = fString.replace('1','T')

fString = fString.replace('0','A')

fString = 'C' + fString + 'C'
```

- **Benefits of using Python**

The script mentioned above can be achieved in C/C++/vb/Java etc. Python has been selected for the purpose of scripting is that python is portable, embeddable and easily extensible.

Python is an interpreted, interactive, object-oriented programming language. It incorporates modules, exceptions, dynamic typing, very high level dynamic data types, and classes.

Python is basically an agile programming language. Further, we don't have to stick to the specific structure and further we can use the powerful features of python interpreter for getting faster response time.

Python combines remarkable power with very clear syntax. It has interfaces to many system calls and libraries, as well as to various window systems, and is extensible in C or C++.

It is also usable as an extension language for applications that need a programmable interface. Finally, Python is portable: it runs on many Unix variants, on the Mac, and on Windows 2000 and later.

Python is a high-level general-purpose programming language that can be applied to many different classes of problems.

The language comes with a large standard library that covers areas such as string processing (regular expressions, Unicode, calculating differences between files), Internet protocols (HTTP, FTP, SMTP, XML-RPC, POP, IMAP, CGI programming), software engineering (unit testing, logging, profiling, parsing Python code), and operating system interfaces (system calls, file systems, TCP/IP sockets). A wide variety of third-party extensions are also available.

In short, we have selected python for script because, we require less response time and more flexibility such that script can be modified at any time easily.

- **Storage and Required Lab Conditions**

The conventional DNA extraction and analysis process require lot of lab apparatus, such as micro pipettes, vials, chemical solution. However, modern techniques claim to complete the DNA extraction in 40 seconds and by chain termination method, shotgun sequencing method and site directed mutagenesis, we can easily get the structure, we require in another one minute.

The single vial can carry the DNA as long as 10 million base pairs or in digital term as long as 10 million bits. If the data exceeds there can be multiple vials that can consist of DNA Data Warehouse.

The important thing here is that the whole process must be performed under controlled lab condition, which includes normal room temperature and the sterility of the environment must be maintained.

- **Challenges**

The whole process of DNA Data warehouse may seem to be very fascinating but in reality there can be series of challenges and lot of research work is required to bring this to reality.

It can be very difficult to maintain the sterility of the environment.

Moreover automation of whole process can be very difficult and expensive during the initial setup of the DNA Data Warehouse.

Following are basic challenges that are faced while dealing with DNA:-

1) Temperature

Unlike any biological material, DNA also survives only in certain range of temperature, usually inside the cell, the temperature stays normal as the room temperature but while DNA is extracted from the cell it is needed to be preserved at minimum of -20 degree centigrade.

However, there have been recent researches where possibilities of preserving DNA at room temperature have also been explored.

2) Storage and Transportation

Other than maintaining sterility of the environment, it is very important to preserve DNA in plastic vials; the DNA must be protected from direct sunlight and warmer conditions.

3) Sterility

We are dealing with DNA for only material purpose but it is very important to make sure, DNA doesn't gets contaminated, DNA is very sensitive material, it can get contaminated with fingerprint, dust etc. it is very important to maintain sterility of the place, where DNA is stored.

4) Bio-Ethics

It has been seen in past, for every new development involving, genes, cells, DNA, or genetically modified organisms, there are many concerns that are raised from the community.

Similar concerns can be raised while implementation of DNA data warehouse, people can get scared on the fact that something with actual life is being used to save the data.

Further, there could be concerns from environment activists, on using living plant, insect or animal for extracting DNA, to be used for material purpose.

Chapter 7

The Way Forward

The purpose of this book is to demonstrate the challenges in dealing with big data and proposing the solution for most important issue of finding a next generation storage material.

This approach will also support the principle of green IT, since DNA is a biological material, it can easily be recycled, as compared to other storage materials, which are either made of silicon or are of plastic base.

In long term, it may also be possible to develop a hard disk made of DNA as a storage material rather than silicon.

The initial setup to use DNA as a storage material may prove costly but in long term, it will lead to development of DNA data warehouse and it will be possible to use DNA as a next generation storage material at very cheap price.